BENITA'S BOOK

William Talcott

Thumbscrew Press
San Francisco
1997

© 1997 William Talcott

Some of the poems (or earlier versions of them) have appeared in the following magazines: *Black Buzzard Review, Blowfish, Convolvulus, Cups, Exquisite Corpse, House Organ, Jejune, Minotaur, Poetry Flash, Poetry USA, 33 Review & Voicefree (Ireland)*.

Cover by Hatem.

Thumbscrew Press
1331 26th Avenue
San Francisco, California, 94122
ISBN: 1-879457-53-9

CONTENTS

1 Crossing the Line
2 Yes
3 The Flow We Get
4 Before the Wedding
5 Mythic Butter
6 Aubade Suite for Evening
8 Sent Saturday
9 It Starts
10 Benita's Book
11 Pas de Deux
12 The Rain
13 Amish Friendship Bread
14 Galleria d' Amore
15 Autumn Feelings
16 Holding Pattern
17 A Scree of Gewgaws
18 The Mile High Club
19 Poem In the Form of a Tooth
20 Recipe for a Pleasant Afternoon
21 Ecology
22 Metamorphosis
24 Fantasy in C Major
25 Exotic
26 At the Drop of a Hat
27 Variation on Paul Eluard
28 Breakup

29 I Understand What You're Doing
30 Polyandry
31 Geriatric Poem
32 The Book
33 Homeric Hymn
34 The Remedies of Love
35 Fetish
36 Fever Dreams
37 Oysters
38 Benita's Smile
39 Butter on a Cat's Paw
40 Dessert
41 Lychee
42 Half the Sun Painted and the Whole Sky
44 Legs
45 Finding You
46 Grassed
47 Prelude
48 Accents
50 Flight
51 Majnun Laila
52 The Island of Doctor Moreau
54 For Michael
55 Moonrise
56 How Rare Things Are
58 Epilogue

BENITA'S BOOK

For Benita

Those warm kisses remain there,
amputated from before and after
existing in their own right
like the frail transparencies of ferns or roses
pressed between the covers of old books.

—Lawrence Durrell, *Balthazar*

Crossing the Line

You wondered why I came by
when I could have used the phone.
Time passed in talk and hints
until I touched your skin
(a finger I think) to find you
connected to my body and my fear.

I read my poems at a coffeehouse.
The invitation included a husband
or a friend. You said *Michael
if he can.* You came alone
in a flower print dress.
When applause thickened the air

I said *let's go* and we went
to the first storefront.
We walked to your car like that,
pausing and kissing, then you
showed me how the front seat worked.
Do you like this? you asked. *God yes.*

Yes

We go shopping for underwear
on our first date. I help you
try on Wonder Bras. We don't
buy them. You choose uplift
shorts for me to get that ballet
dancer definition. Our ears
hold *April in Paris* by Lady Day.
We'll rent by the week
at Place de la Contrescarpe
or just pass through and spend
the whole trip in the sleeper
on the Trans-Siberian Railway.
In this story you'll play
the muse of my being, the muse
for a century of poems.

The Flow We Get

walking by the Bechtel
freight car where your friend
Mike used to work. The PG&E
fountain that hypnotizes.
Deli 123 on Mission and I
introduce you to Frank
my former mentor smiling
that smile of his and saying
your name means *beautiful*.
It doesn't. Same old Frank
always on the sniff but I
say nice things about him
as we move toward Ghandi's
big bronze toe rubbed shiny
by the touchers of this world
including us our shoulders
bumping softly on purpose.
We eat sandwiches and watch
the boats. Did the small one
meant for Sausalito ever leave?
You play that game with me—
I close my eyes and point
to imaginary body parts
that suddenly get wet
when you cheat with your mouth.

Before the Wedding

Strange clouds float through these trees
not knowing whether to become
limes or green flowers.

I hold them briefly in my arms.

I want to hold you but you've
gone with the bride to be painted.

Peach is the palette of the wedding
though the season for them has passed.

The invitation shows two hearts
sprouting little hands to shake the hands
of guests yet to appear.

The harpist tunes her harp.

Sails spike the bay
blending with white-tipped waves
as the fog rises.
                We're headed
toward the horizon, knowing
whatever's there beyond our vision
wants as we move to become *here* for us.
The moment is ours and the desire.

Mythic Butter

I talk because I want to
taste you on the phone.
I stay awake most of the night
watching the blankets beside me
where your body almost sleeps.
I want to stop time to touch
each inch of your skin
in one moment and if I appear
to be on fire it's only because
I want to be with you
in new unusual ways. I don't have to
look in your eyes to know your touch
says more than all these words.

Aubade Suite for Evening

My eyes reflect the blur
of fog that greets the first
wild ducks of fall. We've parted
for the day and I'm doing
what we'd be doing if we hadn't.

The first wild ducks
are on the lake, heading south
or maybe here to stay a while.
The sky over the island hill
is low and uniformly white.
I'll go there in a bit
and lose my eyes
which spent the afternoon
so full of you.

I'm leaning on the railing
of the wooden bridge above
the fake waterfall. Almost
wrote *the wooden bride*.
You're married to another.
I had hoped the fog
would stop my seeing that
but it's not low enough
except for shape shifters
that pass like ghosts.

I'm thirsty and the water
roars like evening traffic.
Two juncos, maybe the ones
we saw together. White
tail feathers either side.

The hooded head.
They play like children
near Sweeney's defunct observatory.
I'm higher now facing west
and here the roar *is* traffic.

The stone bridge to Strawberry Hill
"Erected 1893" inscribed on a slab
so solid, surviving all disasters.
I pause to look for hawks.
I said we'd do that. We might
not find any but we'd
find something if we looked.

Tamarindo for the thirst
at that coffeehouse we went to once.
Last week we shared a glass at Bianco's
between kisses. I felt light
headed as though a barber
from another time had bled me
to cure my madness for your mouth.
Your moisture, this mist
that greets the first
wild ducks of fall.

Sent Saturday
October 29th at 9:01 PM

Hi William this is Benita.

If you are listening to your message
I am at your place.

I am calling from your place.

Just want to let you know.

Come home.

It Starts

with a kiss then your breasts
those small delights of my fingers
twisting their nipples
this way and that as your throat
makes an audible inhale
to tell me to touch your wetness.
You sigh once more.
My thighs between your legs
move the same as yours.
When your lips grow slack
I trace them with my tongue
and know what your body wants.
Your back arches in my arms.
Your eyes close. My name
is written on your lips.

Benita's Book

Dream voices tell me
to write these poems.
What about, candles
dripping wax on your skin?
There'd have to be a bed
and seedless watermelons
at three a.m., the juice
from our mouths on your sheets.
We'll fall asleep kissing.
If your lips get dry
it's their way of telling
me to lick them. We'll lay
on the grass at Yerba Buena Gardens
then kiss behind the waterfall.
All the persimmons you ever peeled
will tinge the clouds at sunset
as its light opens
the latest page from *Benita's Book*.

Pas de Deux

We can't touch. Someone might see.
So we look and speak what we desire.
I say how I would place my hands
and you, what you would do
with your mouth. *Sotto voce*
and our faces dance.

We'd kiss if we could but this
is somehow better. Our eyes' dark centers
widen, our lips, raspberries in rain.
Words we say surround us in a magic
circle as we walk and make believe
no one can see our dance.

The Rain

that fell and added numbers
to the graphs we'll read
tomorrow in the news
has stopped for now. Enough
for me to do a load of wash
and stop by Durty Nelly's for a pint.
I think of you, reservoirs fill.
Hetch Hetchy, Berryessa.
Droughts, like logic
come and go in California
but thoughts of you come on
like some new endorphin
that wets the tip of my existence.
This morning on the phone
I drank your voice and all
the words our skin will say
tomorrow when we touch.

Amish Friendship Bread

I almost followed directions
but kept misplacing the list
you gave me with its do this
day 1, and that, day 6.

You had your list too
and a glob of batter
from the same batch.

The first great spill
glued the phone book shut.
I didn't tell you
till you mentioned the mess
on your persian rug.

We spoke on the phone
how to cook this stuff.
What can I do when fantasies
get wild and your response
gets wilder. So we baked
the bread and brought our loaves
to feed each other
and your delight became
our very cells for seven years
and less than one has passed.

Galleria d'Amore

Now Indian Summer's gone
and the weather turns fierce.
Our words soften to chapped
whispers as we kiss
and we walk uphill backwards
in the wind.
                You have a little
laugh that tells me when I've
pleased you. We've found a place
with no cameras to watch us.
Even the floors shine with love.
Given what's given it's enough.

The year swallows the days.
Let me play the days, you the year.
Let "R" stand for roof garden
and "B" for basement where the vault is.
Here comes the elevator to take us
to our special place where we linger
in our prolonged vertical ways.

Autumn Feelings

When yesterday's rain reaches Utah
I know it's today already.
Clouds smile at that. The air

brightens with an autumn feeling.
A fine day for touching
the person you wake up with.

Today we ate sea urchins
raw then kissed
near the vault of a bank.

I was born over a bank in the East.
You were born during riots in Japan
with all your parts and more.

Some attract my attention
and I want to tease them with those
little love bites you taught me.

Holding Pattern

What word could hold the feeling
you bring my body to? What place?
You say the heart, not with words,
but a gesture near your breasts.
For me it's higher up, near the eyes
I see you with.
                    When we touch
that place moves where all lovers go—
a pasture by the sea, and you can
ride the ponies there and bring them
near sounds of waves that slap the shore.
My hands, your voice.

A Scree of Gewgaws

Haven't read the news in months
then I see on B2 Ella's legs
amputated, wasted from diabetes.
What am I doing with my life
while the jazz age sinks
in a wheelchair and Annie Sprinkle's
having lunch with Margot St. James
back from Paris and the San Jose
Ballet's on its toes. Page B12—
lions, leopards & lynxes, not to mention
some primates, exposed to strong perfumes
became embarrassingly lascivious
at an English zoo. You're also in
my thoughts Benita, your power to heal
imaginary ailments just by smiling.

The Mile High Club

Well not quite.
Only the 36th floor
of the Marriott
that art-deco knockoff
with the marvelous view.

We're so into each other
we can barely eat
the Caesars we ordered.
How many times can we
kiss in public without
attracting an audience?

But look!
Half the floor's
closed off, waiting
for the evening crowd.

So we pay the bill
and walk to the empty
side to touch the view
more delicious than lunch
and neither cold nor dry.

Poem In the Form of a Tooth

The day started with toothy
questions like *when* and *if*
and went on to mention Asian silk
imprinted with white cranes.

Had the lack of fighting teeth
in our ancestors made us soft?
When the mountainside we're
standing on liquefies, we spread

-eagle and ride it down. Call it
an avalanche. Call it love.
They say the view's terrific
when you reach the bottom.

Such small teeth says the lady
dentist from the Argentine.
*Me gustan. Opportunities
for delicate root canals.*

Your mind can make your body rich.
That's what it said inside
the fortune cookie before I bit it.
Mind/body split said the tooth.

Recipe for a Pleasant Afternoon

Remove outer covering and wash.

Test with fingers for firmness
and response.
                Cook slowly
lowering and raising temperature
until moist.
                Add stuffing.

Keep hot over continuous flame
till ready to serve.

Spread on bed of woven
vegetables and cover
with whatever fancies you.

This is a traditional dish
but variations are endless.

Serves two.

Ecology

I'm looking for signs of small
pond life in the backyard
when you come to the window
smiling, cupping your breasts
and dressed in a miraculous bikini
of nothing at all. Is this ecology?
The balance of nature escapes me
but you don't.
I go back up and we make love
like Siamese fighting fish
then take a walk in the park
where I show you my favorite trees.

Metamorphosis

Ovid wrote a book about it.
Gregor Samsa had his problems.

In another movie the hero
a wild wolf all night
turns into a man at dawn
and his girlfriend turns
into a hawk.
        My last
wife called me a slug
when she was pissed
but she was a force
of nature, like salt.

What animal would you be?

Some nut on *Saturday
Night Live* asked Nixon
outside his posh New York
condo. He didn't disappoint
us with an answer.
        I know
what yours would be.
I choose to make no choice.

Today I offered a million
pennies for you to run
away with me.
                     We kissed
at Starbucks when you
recognized that look I get.
Once more in Jesse Alley
cross-street Annie.
Are these our secret names?

Then you opened your coat.

I'm not sure I want
to be an animal at all.

Fantasy in C Major

If the bed squeaks
we'll make love so slowly
the neighbors will strain
to listen. When the big
quake comes, we'll still
be embracing and when
the house falls down
around us, everyone
will see us and marvel
at this great contest
between the shuddering earth
and our bodies which never
get enough of each other.

Exotic

I met you inside myself
like a seed growing there.
The charm
        of the unfamiliar.

Exotica — You
        but not you.
The Abyssinian
        sword lily.
Creamy white blossoms
        blotched
chocolate brown within.

The Nile's an exotic river
        because between
the source and the mouth
it travels through desert.

All that wetness
        flowing
in a hot dry place.

At the Drop of a Hat

A late afternoon sun
burns holes in Spuntino's scrim
casting shadows of my wild hair
like black flames on the wall.

I'm in a holding pattern.
A glass of wine till opera time.
Red spots on a paper napkin.
Thinking of you and how you
wrecked my sheets and me last Friday.

Once by accident you spilled
coffee on my clean shirt
and asked if I would wear
the shirt again for you.
I didn't know you'd notice
but you did, or did I forget
and wear the stained shirt
twice from laziness or fate.

Longing is anticipation in reverse.
I was with you, will be so again
and though this moment
holds your presence, you're not here.
Call me and I will come
at the drop of the hat
I do not wear.

Variation on Paul Eluard

The cheese stands alone.
The mountain shepherd in *Shadows
of Forgotten Ancestors*
lifts it from a pail of milk
and rolls it with his hands
talking all the while.
Clean wood tones by fire light.
Wind and stars outside the cabin.
Below in the valley the beloved.
When I'm not with you
I no longer know
which one of us is absent.

Breakup

I want to see her right away but she refuses. She says later we'll have lunch. I call again and she agrees. She's late and wants to go to the Post Office for three-cent stamps. The line's long and the machines have only one-cent stamps so we get those. Then I persuade her to our secret place we call the *Love Tunnel* where we kiss and touch, then go our separate ways. She says we have to stop. Our lunch will be soup in Chinatown, her continuing to talk about not seeing each other. No love-making anyway which makes me sad because we're good that way together. She loves me she says but has to stay apart to save the marriage. I understand I say then go into a tirade against the husband. Then I tell her the movie plot to *Eat Drink Man Woman* and she smiles. By now people we know arrive. We decide to leave. We still have half an hour, what should we do, visit that church we wanted to see? It's raining. No umbrella. We need shelter. We go back to the *Love Tunnel* and make love. We're not doing well with this break-up thing I say during a kiss. She laughs.

I Understand What You're Doing

I understand why.
What escapes me is how
you can do this thing at all.

One night we slept, our lips
joined in a dream long kiss
much more than table, tea or soup.

To end it is to end this poem
which goes on in my heart
after the words run out.

Polyandry

Women like the idea.
Some have the energy for it.
For most men it's a spider
under the toilet seat.
They're always checking.
Except in the mountains
of Tibet where a good woman
has many husbands but not
in the same house. Do they wear
wedding rings? You didn't
when we met. Your husband
bought you one when you told him
you were practicing polyandry.
Then you took me to a jeweler
to have my finger measured.
Size eight and a half.
I wish we'd bought that ring.

Geriatric Poem

Imagine I'm ninety years old
having trouble breathing.

It's you I want to call
for help but I can't

because your husband
(age sixty-four)

has those *end it all*
feelings again and you

have to tend to him
because you don't

want to *break the family*.
Your son (age thirty-six)

had been by for dinner
to remind you. Benita

(age sixty-seven)
I love you

and I think I'm dying.

The Book

That book on your night table
half-read, yet so full of promise.
Business had intruded like hands
on the face of a clock. The one
in your kitchen, does it have

Roman numerals? I haven't
seen it but I did see you today
upstairs in a cafe and I held
the hand with your wedding ring
or rather it held mine.

Delights there are that do not know us.
Now even that's lost as we enter
this half-read book, waiting
for a newer version of ourselves
to pick it up and finish it.

Homeric Hymn

Thank you Aphrodite
for this day when I

saw Benita and she
touched my hand.

On the elevator
she kissed me

and didn't complain
I had been smoking.

The Remedies of Love

We could have talked more
but when together we wanted
touch and afterward came
hardly any time.
                    *Many things
in my heart to tell you*
Mimi says, dying in La Bohème.
*Just one thing really
my love e tutta la mia vita.*

Last August time flipped
and we lived awhile forever.
To part still loving is surgical.

I went to a bookstore tonight
to buy Ovid's *The Remedies
of Love* and found him saying
man's best friend is his dog.

Love dies a natural death
sometimes. The violent
wrenching we feel for logic
aches unnaturally. If you feel
possible to love without good-byes
tell me and I will until love dies.

Fetish

I'll read some Wyatt
before I go to bed.
I love those *straunge*
words before the rules
made life so *chargéd*
with forgetfulnes.

Then I'll conjure
images of Benita.
When below equals above
and all things have meaning
nothing lacks love.

Unable to contain myself
I pull the nostrils
of the fetish to my mouth
taking deep breaths.

Fever Dreams

The darkness of a great
free to be hungry in
evening when swallows
and bats suck mud
from the barn's eaves
and the twilight's empty
spaces break to shapes
of greasy nothing.

That's the time angels
dream of pleasure
that comes from not eating
too much before love.

Sometimes it helps
to sweat. Then sweat
you say. In this way
lunch is decided.

I have captured
the songs of early
morning and sent them
your way in a letter.

When we love a fine
dust settles over us
as in the pulverization
of Sarajevo, marked by
the footprints of feral cats
and artillery rings wild
bells in the sky.

Oysters

As I walk home
the crescent feels warm
and lazy in the sky.

I just kissed the mouth
that gives birth
to the voice I love to hear.

After two hours with you
I need oysters!

So I go back to P.J.'s
where you dined last week
an hour before I did.

I look around but you've
gone skiing at Squaw and me
I'm always late.

I slurp the oysters
and spit out the pearls

except for yours
which I honored
with my best attentions
only a few hours ago.

Benita's Smile

A door opening
    that has been trying to close.

An invasion of Japan by Kublai Khan.
    A divine wind.

A gold-rimmed plate
    sparking in the microwave.

Images that walk
    across the page that describes them.

Two logs bursting
    into the flame that devours its parents.

The exotic
    she asked me to write about.

Technicolor paisleys dripping down
    a wood-stained wall to Kimio Eto's koto.

Like switching on the ignition
    and nothing happens then you
    suddenly understand what metal means.

Butter on a Cat's Paw

She's closed like a flower
so I give these poems about her
and ask for help with corrections.
She helps.

Whenever I get a new cat
I put butter on its paw. Nervous
at first with the new surroundings.
By the time she licks it clean
she'll be happy she's here.

By week's end I'm stealing
prize roses from the park.
If I'm caught, it's
five hundred dollars a rose.
I take seven.
Each bud opens in her vase.

Dessert

Once again I have dessert
before the main meal

caffe affogato in North Beach
so sweet and strong and later

I'll be wide awake but not
as sweet as you before lunch

and no, since you asked, I didn't
taste a trace of the medicine

you're taking for being positive
on your TB patch test.

Lychee

Break the skin

Enjoy its glistening inner flesh

No rush

I want to watch you

Take it inside your mouth

And let its juices burst

Half the Sun Painted and the Whole Sky

Below is Emerald Bay or the ice
forests of Altair-Nine
and it's raining on three moons.
Brushstrokes of light move down
your arms. Hands by Franz Hals.

All water has a skin
to keep the small moons dry.
Our touches like layers of paint
stir something deeper.
The vanishing point perhaps.

Hyperboles leave our lips
to show everyone we're American.
The neighbors mumble while scanning
the papers for signs of a future
remarkably unknown like our own.

The sky tells me nothing
except how similar we are—
the same number of fingers
the same sensitivity to light
when the barometer tops thirty.

Should our shadows evaporate
we'll find our sweat
bonded to flesh like vernex.
We'll have good posture
to keep our heads above water.

That connection with you
tells me all I need to know.
If the plural of paradox is paradise
I will love you forever
tending to be monogamous.

Legs

If she stopped
to gaze at the menu next door
she'd be quite lovely
but motion destroys the glamour
she's worked so hard for.
You on the other hand
know how to walk.
Your legs enjoy each other.
When you sit
they know their place
and when we're side by side
one may slide over mine
like an old friend
reminding me of other
times we've been together.
Then the Past
lives in the Present
and we don't need the *I Ching*
to know what's going to happen.

Finding You

We put on our clothes
and were off to meet
Michael and his friend
at the party for the new

museum. My damp hair might
look odd if we arrived together
so I lagged at your request.
Then I lost you in the crowd.

I stared from the second
story landing at faces
coming in the door
until I saw kaleidoscopes.

A molecule of air inside
a rainbow. A raindrop
fallen in the Bay.
How could I find those?

Sometimes I find you
unexpectedly. Your height
and profile. Your cut of hair.
I turn and my heart is riding

a sudden drop in pavement
or an airpocket and it rises
and continues to rise
but you aren't there.

Grassed

Grass grows under our bodies.
Blue-eyed with two flowers
that's me, face-down on the green.
It's bright. The sky, I mean, but she's
writing checks, heavy checks for dull
money she frets about and plucks a blade.
She peels back the glume, exposing
soft parts near the root and puts it
in her mouth to suck the sugar there.
She loves to eat but ruminates on money
turquoise and bamboo. She chews.
I feel her next to me, ankle to hip
and churn inside. I turn and grasp
her shoulder to kiss her lips.
Her mouth does not refuse
and fills my mouth with grass.

Prelude

We sit face to face
touching accidentally
then pulling back as we talk.
The clock in some church
strikes five. *We have to
get back now* someone says
as we lean toward each other
our mouths teasing a long fast
but not giving in to the feast.
A sigh fills my ears, and it ends.
I leave for Europe Tuesday.
We're on for lunch Monday.
As we walk you ask *What kind
of lunch do you have in mind?*

Accents

Your voice on the phone.
A kiss. The glow
on my skin beside you
as we head for the Bay
and the Wave Organ
gurgling in its pipes.

Where's the brass plate?
We give up and cross
the street to the Palace
of Fine Arts. Under the big
dome I clap hands once.
Three echos back I'm happy.

By the lagoon a wedding party.
White gowns trailing over dirt.
Cameras flash.

What duck is that?

On the grass you turn
to look me in the eyes.
*You want to touch me
don't you
to see if I'm wet.*

I want to all the way
up Russian Hill and down
Macondray Lane. White star
flowers where the street
should be, then the stairs.

Hands in pockets, dangerous
but at L'Osteria a scoop
of vanilla swims in espresso.
Drowned coffee. You make
bad jokes about forgetfulness
and we laugh at the precious
beach glass earrings
at the fair on Grant Street.

Lobsters wait at Anthony's
on the square. Oysters.
A bowl of clams and mussels.
Mermaids sing as we eat.

To share this day, its accents
holding all fourteen sacraments
of an old religion
only recently discovered.

Flight

I saw your face after the long
sunset when the northern lights
played for an hour then the false
dawn glowed over Labrador.
Now I sit around and watch the monkey
puzzle tree, out of place in the next
yard. Magpies and thrushes. Many crows.

Tonight I sleep in a land of amber drink
and music. You don't like amber but you
liked the opals I gave for your ears.
Do you ever wear them now?

My poems have failed, Benita.
Here in Ireland the Druid bards
had power to rhyme a man to death.
My poems can't get you out
of the house unless you want to.

At the pub I'll see the puppet
master who once eloped with a nun.
Maybe I'll talk to the actor from Bray
who had that bit part in *Braveheart*.
Is that all there is? asks the widow
after a one line poem on marriage.

Majnun Laila

Your first kiss. Wish
it had been me. Only you
know the reason and I
will never tell. Majnun
didn't say that. I did.

But when he saw her
by the well without her veil
her father made her marry
someone else.
              Then he went
to the desert and prayed for sleep
to dream making love to Laila
writing poem after poem for her only.
He lost his name which was nothing
and his love lived in legend
a thousand years.
              Like Majnun
I will go to my dreams
to find you and give the lie
to the desert I wake to.

The Island of Doctor Moreau

Words that abstract
time abstract me and I forget
who I am. Elephants
prevent the bar rail
from falling. They work
as a team like the nipples
of the woman in the white chemise.
I must stop looking at them
so perfectly centered, the lights
switched on at my birth.
Time's no metronome
and the stories everyone rewrites
have the halitus of something
familiar, the silly season
frothing under a freshening breeze.

Before your name's on my lips
I hear whispers
and before the whispers
a hint of evening
moves silently through the curtains.
If we lose our shadows, it's not
that we're characters in one of
Hoffman's tales. We're indoors
with the lights out, part
of a community of objects
without shadow or rather
one shadow, all colors the same.
Here I will paint your portrait.
Unexpected noises are the house
settling or mice
rummaging in the sideboard.

The cloth over the cage
of Dante the parrot
gauges the overkill of dreams.
I too turn into a beast
after some complaining.
Take away hope
I become polite again
and kind to myself.
Time does that anyway.
Not to wake up beside you
drills me to a here and now
otherwise filled with books
and the movement of stars
through so many minutes and hours.
I learn their names.
Alnitak, Alnilam, Mintaka.

For Michael

His hand gripped mine at the hospice
after I told him about Paris
during the strike and seeing
The Marriage of Figaro in
Mozart's Prague. Now he's gone.

Here in Portland birches weep
by the Tudor house across the street.
Mount Hood hides behind a stand of poplars.
No one could see it anyway in this rain.
At the Green Room where I sit
drums and bass set up the trumpet's jazz
alive and full of contradictions

like you, Benita. You loved Michael
so I think of you also and the loss
of one who cared for you
and opera and Paris. Mike and I
didn't know each other as both
of us knew you, but if I
measure a man by what he loved
my world is less for his leaving.

Moonrise

The moon rises behind us.
We're watching the sun
sink in the off-shore fog
hoping for the mythic
green flash.
Later the moon
makes shadows of us both.
Till then we look
at the dissolving sun
and forgive with one touch
everything that has disappointed us.

How Rare Things Are

Wolves howled as Zhivago
wrote his poems for Lara.
Had she been you I would
have made that journey
to the east.

Feeling must be cousin
to the moistures of the earth
connected in some way
to cum and tears
and we are water signs
so we should know.

Will I know you in a month?
I'm not sure. Yet something
tells me this unfinished
thing between us won't end
in ways that we can script.

So much I wanted to say.
You said the same.
Tomorrow we may love.
How rare things are.

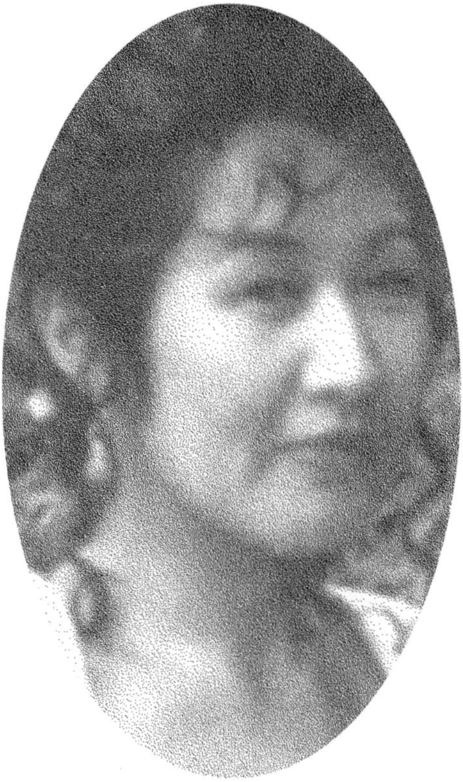

Epilogue

I could have said more about you, Benita.
We'd buy lychees at a little shop in Chinatown
and eat them as we walked, peeling
off the skin, spitting seeds in the street.

Taste this, it is liver. I tasted.
It is not liver, you said, *it is lung.*
Three tongues in your head—
you do not use contractions in your speech.

Your father played dance band trumpet
in Hawaii before the War and joined the Army
for the easy life. Went home with them
to the Philippines to survive Bataan.

After the war he went to Japan and took
his revenge by taking their women— his joke
to your mother, who gave you long limbs
and taught you how to juggle.

You tan easily and do not like sun in your eyes.
Kids in Japan called you *kurombo* to tease you.
Well-connected in your body, you pumped iron
at Gold's Gym even in your eighth month.

Your father died at ninety
after calling you on the phone.
Sometimes you refer to him
as though he were still alive.

Of your marriage I say nothing
except you felt its harmony
disrupted by our passion.
Your *logic* closed your heart.

Sometimes I think Benita was a fiction
like Laura or Lesbia. The opals
I gave her, the many flowers.
In my dreams she is also dreaming.

This book was set in Sabon, designed by Jan Tschichold, and Gill Sans, designed by Eric Gill. It was printed at the West Coast Print Center in Berkeley, California.